ARCHIMEDES:

Greatest Scientist of the Ancient World

by

D.C. Ipsen

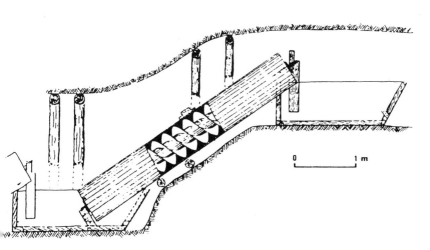

Drawing of an Archimedes' screw unearthed in an ancient Roman mine in Spain.

ENSLOW PUBLISHERS, INC.

Bloy St. & Ramsey Ave.   P.O. Box 38
Box 777   Aldershot
Hillside, N.J. 07205   Hants GU12 6BP
U.S.A.   U.K.

Library of Congress Cataloging-in-Publication Data

Ipsen, David C.
    ARCHIMEDES: Greatest Scientist of the Ancient World
    Bibliography: p.
    Includes index.
    Summary: Traces the life and discoveries of the Greek
mathematician, scientist, and inventor, sometimes called
'the father of experimental science.'
    1. Archimedes–Juvenile literature. 2. Scientists–
Greece–Biography–Juvenile literature. [1. Archimedes.
2. Mathematicians. 3. Scientists] I. Title.
Q143.A62I67 1989   509.2'4 [B]   [92]   88–31006
    ISBN 0-89490-161-3

Printed in the United States of America

10 9 8 7 6 5 4 3 2

ILLUSTRATION CREDITS:
Azienda Autonoma Turismo-Siracusa, pp. 11, 47; David C. Ipsen,
pp. 22, 33, 35, 58; Leonardo da Vinci. *I Libri di Meccanica*, p. 514.
Milano: Ulrico Hoepli, 1940, p. 7; Reproduced by courtesy of the
Institution of Mining and Metallurgy from *Trans. Instn Min. Metall.*,
36, 1926-27, 199-336, p.1.

Contents

Preface 4

1. Earth Mover 5

2. Naked Truth 10

3. Balancing Act 18

4. Egyptian Interlude 25

5. Squaring the Circle 30

6. A Sandy Universe 37

7. Time of War 43

8. Blood and Sand 50

9. Life after Death 53

Glossary 59

Further Reading 62

Index 63

Preface

Although I might have trouble convincing everybody that he was the greatest scientist of all time, calling Archimedes the greatest scientist of the ancient world should bring few objections, even though he lived in an age of great thinkers. And certainly his range of brilliant performance—from the discovery of mathematical relations to the establishment of physical laws to the design of equipment for war and peace—has been unmatched in any age.

Writing about Archimedes is frustrating because of the many gaps and uncertainties in our knowledge of the man and his activities. Most of his scientific works have survived, but descriptions of how and when he created them have not. And descriptions of his feats as an experimenter or a designer are largely hearsay. Anyone who wants to know about the achievements of Archimedes must choose which stories to believe and which to reject. I have tried to give the reader that choice, though I have not always hidden my own views.

I am indebted to Owen Gingerich, Professor of Astronomy and the History of Science at Harvard, for a helpful review of the manuscript.

1

Earth Mover

"Give me a place to stand and I'll move the world!"

It was a fanciful promise, of course, but it was made by a man who would gain fame for feats that sounded almost as impossible. The man was Archimedes, the brightest star of ancient Syracuse.

The person who heard the boast was a man of some fame himself. He was noted for being a peace-loving ruler in a time when rulers were often warlike. King Hiero II ruled Syracuse from 270 B.C. to 216 B.C., a span that covered most of Archimedes' adult life. The king and his famous subject were probably related in some fashion. But whether kinsmen or not, they were surely good friends.

King Hiero, intrigued with the idea of moving great objects with small forces, begged his clever friend to stay on earth but still show how he might bring off such a feat.

The tale, not written down till three centuries later, may have grown with the telling. Archimedes and King Hiero, the story goes, went to a beach where a band of men were straining to haul ashore a three-masted ship. Between the prow of the ship and a nearby pier Archimedes attached an arrangement of ropes and pulleys. He then pulled gently with his hand. The ship, so hard to beach before, now moved smoothly toward him—"as if," the teller of the story said, "it were passing over the sea."

Dragging a three-masted ship up on the shore would seem enough of a feat. But the writer insisted that Archimedes first loaded the ship with its usual crew and cargo. After the demonstration, King Hiero was reported to have called out, "From this day forth Archimedes is to be believed in everything that he may say."

The idea of mechanical advantage—getting more force out than you put in—must have been old by Archimedes' time. Surely people had learned years before to use levers to move large weights with small forces. And pulleys had been around long enough that someone could easily have stumbled onto the notion of getting a mechanical advantage from a pulley as well. But Archimedes went beyond anything done before.

A single pulley would have given Archimedes a mechanical advantage of two. By tying a rope to the pier and then running it through a pulley attached to the prow of the ship, he could have doubled the pull on the ship. Of course, merely doubling the force would hardly have been enough. But Archimedes is given credit for figuring out how to use a number of pulleys to double the force again and again.

To do so, Archimedes would have needed to attach pulleys to the pier as well as to the ship. He could then run the rope back and forth a number of times, each time doubling the force. Such an arrangement of pulleys and rope is often called a block and tackle, for the pulleys at each end are usually mounted inside a blocklike object.

Adding pulleys, though, can't go on forever. The friction involved in turning added pulleys soon begins to cut into whatever advantage you get from them. You eventually reach the point where adding a pulley gives less force rather than more.

Engineers who have looked into the matter seem to agree that Archimedes could probably not have done better than to attach three pulleys to the prow of the ship. Ideally, that would have given him a mechanical advantage of six. So for every pound he pulled, the ship would feel at most six—actually less because of friction.

Able to do the work of no more than six people, Archimedes could hardly have moved a large ship—particularly with a gentle pull. Some historians have suggested that the story is probably true except for the size and load of the ship. A block and tackle could certainly move a smaller, lighter craft—and still impress the king.

But others have looked for another answer. The block and tackle is not the only labor-saver that Archimedes is sup-

Leonardo da Vinci, famous painter of the *Mona Lisa,* also drew a picture of a block and tackle. (His design, shown here, has a mechanical advantage of four.)

7

posed to have invented. Some historians, anxious to make the ancient story hold up, have suggested that he may also have used some of his other inventions.

One early writer gives Archimedes credit for inventing the windlass. Since a windlass is simply a crank-and-axle arrangement such as is commonly used for raising a bucket from a well, you would think that somebody would have invented it before Archimedes came along. But the simplest of devices may go undiscovered for centuries. If Archimedes had used a windlass to pull on his block and tackle, he could have increased the mechanical advantage considerably.

Archimedes is also thought to have invented the worm gear. In that device, a screwlike "worm" meshes with the teeth of a gear, giving a large mechanical advantage. If Archimedes had used a worm gear to drive the windlass, he could have increased the mechanical advantage still more. In fact, one historian has calculated that with block and tackle, windlass, and worm gear together, Archimedes could probably have done the job he was supposed to have done.

It is surprising how little is known about the life of Archimedes. Many legends such as this one have survived, often showing signs of improvement with age. And his mathematical feats are mostly well recorded, for he wrote of these himself. But he never wrote about his life. Nor did anyone else have much to say about it. The only biography known to have been written in his time is lost.

The few personal comments about Archimedes that have survived are of a sort that can't be wholly trusted, for they make him sound like the traditional eccentric scientist. He often became so wrapped up in a problem, it was reported, that he forgot to eat—like Isaac Newton centuries later—or to bathe. And when newly bathed and oiled, he is said to have traced diagrams on his oily body as he pondered some weighty mathematical problem. That reminds one of the modern physicist who grabs his ballpoint pen to scribble equations on the palm of his hand.

One event of Archimedes' life that was well recorded was the end of it. His death came suddenly and sadly in 212 B.C Since he was thought to be about seventy-five years old at the time of that tragedy, historians have set 287 B.C as his birth date—but always with a question mark. It is also known that he was the son of an astronomer named Phidias. That we learn because Archimedes mentions his stargazing father in one of his works.

Archimedes' birth, like his death, came in Syracuse, which in those days was an important city in the Greek world. Its location on the eastern coast of Sicily put it close to Rome and to Carthage, two empires that would compete for control of the city during Archimedes' lifetime.

Although he spent most of his life in Syracuse, Archimedes ventured at least as far from home as Alexandria, on the southern shore of the Mediterranean. Located in the delta of the Nile, Alexandria was then another important city in the Greek world, famed as a center of scientific study. Possibly he lived there for a matter of years.

Archimedes may have returned later to northern Africa to apply his engineering talent to building dikes or other means of regulating the Nile. He may also have traveled to Spain, where he was said to have designed an apparatus for spewing burning pitch on enemy ships. But too little is known to be sure of either of these exploits.

Almost any story of Archimedes, it seems, must be taken with a sprinkle of doubt. He did many marvelous things, but some of the most marvelous may never have happened. He never moved the world with his block and tackle, of course—nor perhaps even a three-masted ship. But there can be no doubt that he did move the world, in a figurative sense, with his brilliant and ingenious ideas.

2

Naked Truth

Archimedes' home town of Syracuse is a city that has had its ups and downs. In modern times its remnants of the past hardly suggest its former grandeur. A century ago its population was around twenty thousand. Today it has attracted many more people, but it is still well below its size in Archimedes' time. In those days as many as half a million people lived there. King Hiero could boast, in fact, that his was the largest Greek city in the ancient world.

In earliest times Syracuse was a craggy island close to the mainland of Sicily inhabited by an Italian tribe known as the Sicels. But in 733 B.C., five centuries before Archimedes' time, the Sicels were driven from the island by invaders from Corinth in southern Greece, who set up a permanent settlement. Eventually the Greeks connected the island to the mainland by a causeway, which was later replaced by a bridge.

Over the centuries Syracuse expanded. And as it became a more attractive prize, it was fortified against attack. By the time of Archimedes, the island where the city started had become a well-protected inner city, and massive walls also protected an outer city on the mainland.

Syracuse was governed democratically at times. But often the reins were in the hands of a single ruler such as Archimedes' kinsman Hiero, who took his name from a man who had ruled two centuries earlier.

Hiero, whose life would greatly affect Archimedes', became known as a peace-loving ruler. But he began as a warrior. While he was still a young man, the ruling citizens of Syracuse made him general of the armed forces of the city. The job, he discovered, brought with it a pesky problem. Although many of the men he commanded were citizens of Syracuse, a sizable number were mercenaries—men who had no loyalty to Syracuse but fought simply for pay. By the time Hiero became their commander, the mercenaries had grown unhappy and mutinous and were likely to cause trouble.

Archimedes' home town of Syracuse as it appears today.

Hiero's solution gained him fame in the ancient world, but by today's standards it was certainly ruthless. He led an expedition against an army that was threatening the safety of Syracuse. But his operation was entirely a sham. He first assembled the mercenaries to attack the enemy from one direction. Then he assembled the Syracusan soldiers some distance away to attack the enemy from another direction. Just before the battle began, Hiero quickly retreated with the men of Syracuse, leaving the unsuspecting mercenaries to be destroyed. Freed of the rebellious mercenaries, Hiero quickly rebuilt his forces with men more to his liking. He then attacked the foe in earnest, severely defeating them.

Upon Hiero's victorious return, he was made king of Syracuse. It was the beginning of a fifty-four-year reign that would prove to be a golden age for Syracuse. Hiero is reported to have ruled "without killing, exiling, or injuring a single citizen." In spite of building temples, a theater, and new fortifications, when Hiero died at the age of ninety he left a full treasury. And he accomplished that, according to reports, without heavy taxes.

Once Hiero came to power, his first act was to present his favorite temple with a gift in gratitude for his success—just in case the gods had been helping. The gift was a golden stephane (pronounced like the name Stephanie). Often seen on Greek statues of goddesses, a stephane is a headband that is widest over the forehead and becomes narrower toward the sides of the head. Stories about this golden headdress that Hiero offered to his gods commonly refer to it as a crown, though it was certainly not the sort of crown that one sees on the head of a modern monarch.

Hiero had ordered that the crown be made of pure gold. But he suspected that the goldsmith had substituted some less costly metal, such as gold mixed with silver or copper. Perhaps he had even gold-plated a much cheaper metal. That last possibility could easily have been checked by scratching the crown, except that damaging a sacred object even slightly was out of the question.

Here was a problem worthy of his kinsman Archimedes. How could he discover whether the crown was really gold without doing it any damage? If historians are right about his time of birth, Archimedes was still in his teens at the time Hiero was named king of Syracuse. The king's problem might have been solved by a teenage Archimedes, though the usual story does give the impression of an older man. Of course, who's to say Archimedes wasn't eighty-five or ninety when he died, rather than seventy-five, putting his age at the beginning of King Hiero's reign at around thirty? It's also possible that the king was celebrating some later event.

As the well-known story goes, Archimedes pondered the problem as he relaxed in the public baths of Syracuse. The answer came to him in a flash of inspiration. Some suggest that the inspiration came from noticing the water that overflowed as he lowered himself into the bath. Whatever the source, he leapt from the bath and dashed home through the streets of Syracuse shouting, "Eureka!" Of course, in a colossal display of absentmindedness, he quite forgot to put on his clothes before making his famous dash.

Great thinkers seem often to be remembered more for actions than thoughts. The English scientist Isaac Newton is remembered for being struck by a falling apple. The Italian scientist Galileo is remembered for dropping objects from Pisa's leaning tower. So naturally Archimedes is remembered for streaking naked through the streets of Syracuse. And his most famous statement will always be the cry of "Eureka!", a Greek word which now has a familiar meaning in our own vocabulary: "I have found it!"

Historians tell us that the events we associate with Newton and Galileo probably never happened. Newton, they argue, was struck only with the notion of a falling apple, not the apple itself. Galileo, they insist, only thought about what would happen to objects dropped from the tower of Pisa. But Archimedes' action has rarely been doubted.

Historians, though, have had many doubts about what Archimedes had found. He surely had thought of a way of testing Hiero's crown without damaging it. But there are several ways he might have gone about it. And unfortunately—as with almost anything practical—Archimedes neglected to write down what he did.

The first description we have is from a Roman architect who lived two or three centuries after the time of Archimedes. The architect failed to reveal his source, which could easily have been his own imagination. His idea was that Archimedes got hold of a lump of gold and a lump of silver each the same weight as the crown. He then compared the volume of the three objects: the gold, the silver, and the crown.

This he did by filling a jug with water to the brim, then dropping each of the objects in turn into the jug, causing the water to overflow. To find how much water overflowed, he measured how much water was needed to refill the jug to the brim after each object was removed.

Gold is nearly twice as heavy as silver. So the lump of gold took up not much more than half as much space as the lump of silver. That meant that Archimedes would need around half as much water to refill the jug after removing the gold lump than after removing the silver lump.

The test of the crown was then simple. If it displaced the same amount of water as the lump of gold, it was almost sure to be gold as well. If it displaced more water, it must be some lighter metal. And lighter was almost bound to mean cheaper. Of the metals known to the ancients, only costly platinum was

14

heavier than gold. Mixing gold with any other metal was almost certain to make it lighter.

Measuring the lump of silver as well as the lump of gold supposedly gave a way to find the proportions of those two metals in the crown—if those were the only metals present. But this idea would have worked only if atoms of gold and silver take up the same amount of space when mixed together as when apart.

The scheme described by the Roman architect sounds so simple and foolproof that many historians have decided it must be the one Archimedes used. Of course, it doesn't seem brilliant enough to excite a great thinker such as Archimedes. Could it really have inspired his naked dash through the streets of Syracuse? But there's an old idea of science suggested by William of Occam in the fourteenth century: The simplest explanation is probably the best. Don't complicate matters if you don't have to.

But as it happens, the architect's simple scheme probably would not have worked. If you get a lump of gold or silver weighing the same as the crown (which was actually a rather light headband) and dip it into a jug wide enough to take the crown, you'll probably discover that the surface of the water merely bulges up a bit. If any water does overflow, the small amount needed to refill the jug will be hard to measure with any accuracy. Even with a fair-sized crown, the method would not have given Archimedes an answer he could trust.

It is quite possible that Archimedes tried such a method and found it useless. Only then did he stroll downtown for a bath, perhaps with the look of deep thought already glazing his eyes. And only after he was struck with that great idea we now call Archimedes' Principle—which solves the problem much more neatly—did he leap from the bath with the cry of "Eureka!" on his lips.

An object in a fluid is buoyed up by a force equal to the

weight of the fluid it displaces. Archimedes' Principle is as simple as that. Archimedes' body, as he lolled in the bath, took the place of two or three cubic feet of water. So it was buoyed up by a force equal to the weight of that much water. If he had expanded his chest, his body would have taken up more space and he would have felt a larger buoyant force.

This idea gave Archimedes a simple—and accurate—way to test Hiero's crown. Since gold takes up less space than a lighter metal, it is buoyed up less if submerged in water. So Archimedes could have weighed the lumps of gold and silver in and out of water to see how much weight they lost because of the buoyancy of the water. He could then have done the same with the crown to see how it compared.

A look at the numbers shows how easily he could have uncovered any fraud. Gold is about nineteen times as heavy as water. So a lump of gold will lose one nineteenth of its weight when dipped into water. Silver is only eleven times as heavy as water. So a lump of silver will lose one eleventh of its weight. Such changes in weight could easily be measured by any reasonable balance.

Actually, Archimedes could have made a quick test without any measurement at all. He could have balanced the crown against a lump of gold, hanging the two objects from opposite ends of a horizontal stick. (They wouldn't even have to be the same weight, as long as they were properly balanced.) Then he could have lowered both into a tub of water. If both were gold, the balance wouldn't change. Each would lose the same fraction of its weight. But if the crown were made of a lighter metal, the balance would be upset. The lump of gold, being denser, would plunge deeper.

King Hiero's crown, as it turned out, was apparently not pure gold. Just what alloy the goldsmith had used wasn't reported. Also, what happened to the goldsmith—and to the crown—isn't known.

Ironically, a modern goldsmith making a golden crown would probably never consider making it of pure gold. Gold jewelry today is usually made of fourteen-karat gold or the like, which sounds like gold but is far from it. Since pure gold is twenty-four karat, a crown made of fourteen-karat gold would contain only a little more than half gold. The rest would usually be copper and silver in the right amounts to keep a gold color—or perhaps to make a more desirable one. The ancient goldsmith, like his exposer, was simply ahead of his time.

Archimedes' test of the crown—however he did it—gave him yet another "first." He has been given credit for coming up with the idea of specific gravity. Before he came along, scientists were puzzled about how to describe how dense a substance is. Specific gravity does that. It is simply the weight of a substance relative to water. Gold, being nineteen times as heavy as water, has a specific gravity of nineteen. Silver has a specific gravity of eleven. For Archimedes, specific gravity was a handy idea to use in talking about buoyancy. He showed that any substance with a specific gravity greater than one will sink in water, any substance with a specific gravity less than one will float. Archimedes' idea of specific gravity, like his idea about buoyancy, continues to be useful.

3

Balancing Act

Sometimes a scientist seems to be talking to someone who appears on the scene only many years—possibly centuries—later. When the astronomer Hipparchus in the second century B.C. talked, for example, it was the astronomer Ptolemy in the second century A.D. who eventually listened. Archimedes' listener came not three centuries later, as with Hipparchus, but eighteen centuries later. When Archimedes spoke, it was often the sixteenth-century scientist Galileo who listened.

It is no surprise, then, that the first to decide that Archimedes must have used buoyancy to test Hiero's crown was the famed scientist from Pisa. The first thing Galileo did after quitting medicine for science was to write a paper showing a balancing technique that Archimedes could have used to solve the problem of the crown with the aid of buoyancy.

Galileo, like others who had worried about the problem, supposed that the crown was made of a simple mixture of gold and silver. To find out what mixture, he proposed balancing a lump of gold, a lump of silver, and the crown against the same counterweight before and after lowering the three objects into a jug of water. Measurements of how much the counterweight had to be moved to restore the balance would then reveal the proportions of gold and silver in the crown.

Galileo even went as far as describing in detail how to build a lever from which to hang the objects and the counterweight, and how to measure the change in the counterweight's position. Unfortunately he did not report using such an apparatus himself to see how well it would have worked for Archimedes. There can be little doubt, though, that it would have worked beautifully.

Of course, Galileo's scheme requires an understanding of the law of the lever. But here Archimedes was well equipped. For he wrote about the lever and showed how the weights that it carries are related.

On a seesaw, which is the simplest sort of lever, a person who is half as heavy as the person on the other end can balance the greater weight by sitting twice as far from the pivot. A person a third as heavy can balance by sitting three times as far from the pivot. The weight times the distance from the pivot always matches. This basic law of the lever may well have been known even before Archimedes. But he was the first to prove it.

Archimedes' proof was simple but ingenious. He imagined that two weights that were positioned according to the law of the lever could be broken up into a number of equal parts—as could be done with stacks of coins, for example. Then he moved the parts—the coins, let's say—in a way that didn't change the balance. For example, he moved one coin as far to the left as he moved another to the right. Such a move, he decided, would not make any difference to the lever.

Following this notion he was able to move the coins until they formed a continuous row stretching the same distance on each side of the pivot. Since they were balanced in the end, he decided the coins must have been balanced at the start, for he had done nothing to change the balance.

Archimedes went on to show that the law of the lever holds even when the two weights can't be treated as stacks of coins. For any weights that balance, the weight times the distance from the pivot always matches.

From balancing weights against one another, Archimedes went on to balancing parts of objects against one another. In that way he was able to find the balance point, or center of gravity, of various shapes. When an object is supported at its center of gravity, the weight on one side of the center balances the weight on the other side, just as on a seesaw.

For some shapes the center of gravity is obvious. The center of gravity of a circle is its center. The center of gravity of a square or a rectangle is the point where lines drawn between the corners cross.

For a triangle the result is also simple, but less obvious. Archimedes discovered that you can find the center of gravity of any triangle by drawing lines from each corner to the center of the opposite side. The point where the lines cross is the center of gravity.

Archimedes also found the center of gravity of a segment of a parabola, a more challenging task. A parabola is a curve often glimpsed in sports. Although Archimedes probably didn't know it, the path taken by the discus of the ancient Greek games is a parabola, as is the path of any ball launched into the air—as long as the air doesn't alter the course. A segment of a parabola is then the space you enclose if you join the opposite sides of a parabola with a straight line. Archimedes found not only the center of gravity but the area as well.

Archimedes went on to wonder about a paraboloid, which is the bowllike shape you get if you spin a parabola on its

20

nose. The giant reflecting telescope on Mount Palomar has the shape of a paraboloid. So, roughly, does the reflector in a flashlight. If you put a flat top on the open end of a parabolid, the space you enclose is a segment of a paraboloid. Archimedes found the center of gravity and the volume of such a segment, though his work has been lost. We know of these feats only from the reports of other men of the times.

Archimedes' investigations of levers and centers of gravity—and of buoyancy—were the start of the science of mechanics, which is the study of forces and the effects they have. Mechanics continues to be an important part of modern science.

Archimedes put the new science to work on the practical problem of deciding whether a floating object will float upright or overturn.

Deciding whether a floating object will stay upright or overturn is rather easy—or so it sounds. You simply look at the force of gravity and the force of buoyancy when the object is tipped and decide whether the two forces will tend to right the object or to tip it further. But to locate these two forces, you need Archimedes' ideas about centers of gravity.

Gravity acts downward on every particle of the object. But its effect can often be shown as a single force acting downward through the center of gravity of the object.

Buoyancy acts on the surface of the object that touches the liquid. But its effect, too, can often be shown as a single force. That force acts upward through the center of gravity of the liquid that was displaced by the object. That point is usually called the center of buoyancy.

If the object is a symmetrical boat, the center of gravity and the center of buoyancy lie one above the other, and so the weight of the boat and the buoyancy of the liquid are nicely balanced.

21

But the big question is what happens when the boat is tipped. Usually both the center of gravity and the center of buoyancy move when the boat moves. If the center of gravity moves to the left when the boat is tipped to the left, the boat will overturn unless the center of buoyancy moves leftward too. In fact, to keep the boat from tipping more, the center of buoyancy must move farther to the left than the center of gravity.

The object that most attracted Archimedes' interest was a segment of a paraboloid—the shape for which he had found the volume and center of gravity. Possibly he decided that was as close as he could get, mathematically, to something resembling the hull of a ship. More likely, though, he wasn't thinking seriously about ships, for he looked at the paraboloid when it was floating with its top down as well as up.

Archimedes had a chance to use his ideas about overturning on at least one ship, though no evidence remains that he actually did. According to reports, Archimedes was enlisted

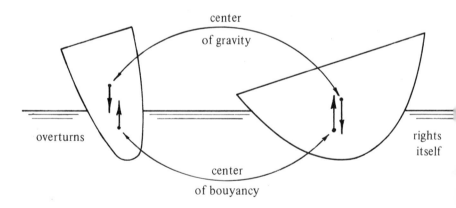

Archimedes' study of floating paraboloids showed how to find when a ship will overturn.

by King Hiero to supervise the building of an extraordinary vessel.

The lowest level had enough room for cargo to make Archimedes' ship the largest cargo carrier of its time. But it was much more than an oversize freighter.

The mid level, location of the cabins and the galley, featured mosaic floors that told the story of the Trojan War—hardly the fittings of an ordinary carrier.

The top level was for recreation—of both body and soul. For the good of the body, the *Lady of Syracuse,* as the splendid craft was named, sported a gymnasium and a bath with bronze tubs. For the good of the soul, it provided walkways through a profusion of plants, some grown to shield any stroller from the Mediterranean sun. It also carried a boxwood-paneled library with a domed ceiling.

The showpiece of the vessel was a lavish shrine to Aphrodite, goddess of love. The floor of the shrine was of beautiful stones, the walls and ceiling of cypress, and the doors of ivory and fragrant cedar. Paintings, statues, and drinking cups served as decoration.

More art decorated the exterior of the craft. A row of larger-than-life statues ran around the perimeter, and paintings covered the sides.

Six hundred oarsmen gave the *Lady of Syracuse* propulsion, though it carried three masts as well. Archimedes equipped the ship with various arms to protect it from attack. Eight turrets held warriors who could shower any attacking vessel with arrows or rocks. According to reports, a large catapult mounted on the ship could hurl stones weighing three talents or javelins measuring twelve cubits. Historians have decided that a talent amounted to around 58 pounds (26 kilograms), making the stones about 175 pounds (80 kilograms). A cubit, the distance from the elbow to the fingertips, varied throughout the ancient world, but was roughly a foot and a half (almost half a meter), making the javelins about eighteen feet or six meters long.

Archimedes is supposed to have launched the ship with the help of a few men, using a windlass. Some historians wonder whether it was the launching of this ship that led to Archimedes' boast that he could move the world.

Hiero planned to use the ship in service between Syracuse and Alexandria and other Mediterranean ports. But he found the ship too large for the ports of call, and he was forced to scrap his grand idea. In a gesture in keeping with the extravagant enterprise, he filled the hold with the plentiful grain from the fields around Syracuse, along with salted fish, and sent the ship as a gift to Alexandria, then suffering from a drought. For its voyage across the Mediterranean, Hiero renamed the vessel *Lady of Alexandria.*

Although Archimedes is supposed to have launched the *Lady of Syracuse,* no story suggests that he beached the *Lady of Alexandria* after its passage across the Mediterranean. But Archimedes visited Alexandria at least once, and it is possible that he made one trip on the great vessel he helped to build.

4

Egyptian Interlude

How long Archimedes stayed in Alexandria is unknown, but it was long enough to make good friends of several scientists he would keep in touch with during his years in Syracuse.

Founded by Alexander the Great less than fifty years before Archimedes' birth, Alexandria had quickly become known as a center of learning. One of its earliest residents was Euclid, who is famous for his works on geometry. Euclid probably died shortly before Archimedes was born.

Still living in Alexandria during Archimedes' time was a somewhat later resident named Aristarchus, who was twenty or so years older than Archimedes. Aristarchus hailed from the Greek island of Samos, which lies off the coast of what is now Turkey. If Archimedes didn't know the man, he at least became quite familiar with his work, which was brilliant.

Only one work of Aristarchus's has survived. In it he shows how to find the size and distance of the sun and the moon. Aristarchus did the job with only a few observations: the length of the zodiac covered by the sun and the moon, the width of the moon compared to the earth's shadow as observed during an eclipse of the moon, and the angle between the sun and the moon when exactly half of the moon's face is lit by the sun.

The last of the observations gave him his biggest news, revealing that the sun was eighteen to twenty times as far away as the moon. The result was far from the truth but was accepted for centuries. Not until the sixteenth century was it questioned, and not until the seventeenth century did anyone check his method and find it inaccurate because of the great distance of the sun.

The firmest friend Archimedes made in Alexandria was a man named Conon, who also came from Samos. Archimedes had great respect for Conon's ability and often sent his latest ideas to him to find out what he thought of them.

Conon is remembered today mostly for naming one of the constellations that we still use in sorting out the stars. It all began when Berenice, wife of the ruler of Alexandria, dedicated a lock of her hair in a temple to ensure the safe return of her husband from an expedition. When the hair disappeared from the temple, Conon suggested it was carried to the heavens and put among the stars. Since then, Coma Berenices—"Berenice's Hair"—has kept its place above Virgo in the northern sky. Berenice was herself to suffer an ugly fate. When her husband died several years later, she was promptly murdered by their ambitious son.

Archimedes also made a friend of Eratosthenes, who ran the famous library of Alexandria. Eratosthenes, a native of Cyrene (now Shahhat, Libya), is remembered for his remarkable estimate of the earth's circumference. He had learned that on the first day of summer the noonday sun reflected from the water in a deep well in the city of Syene (now Aswan) 5,000 stades up in the Nile from Alexandria. That meant the sun must at that moment be directly overhead. On the same day of the year Eratosthenes measured the sun's noonday elevation in Alexandria and found it to be a little more than seven degrees to the south of overhead. If the earth's surface curved that much in 5,000 stades, he figured, the whole circumference must be about 250,000 stades. Although a stade is commonly taken to be somewhat larger, Eratosthenes' stade is believed to have been about a tenth of a mile (a sixth of a kilometer). That puts the earth's circumference at 25,000 miles (40,000 kilometers)—roughly what we know it to be today.

Possibly Archimedes also encountered Apollonius during his visit to Alexandria. Though born in Perga, a town in the south of what is now Turkey, Apollonius apparently spent much of his life in Alexandria. But he was about twenty-five years younger than Archimedes and might well have arrived after Archimedes had departed. Apollonius is remembered today for the work he did on conics, those curves you get when you cut a cone. In the course of his work he introduced the words *ellipse, parabola,* and *hyperbola,* still used to name such curves.

Even though they may not have met, Apollonius and Archimedes knew about each other's work. In fact, the younger scientist is said to have annoyed Archimedes by outdoing him in several of his feats. For example, when Archimedes invented a simple way to describe large numbers, Apollonius pointed out a simpler way. Such annoyances, the story goes, led Archimedes to challenge Apollonius with a difficult problem known today as the Cattle Problem.

As any student of Greek mythology knows, the sun god Helios once kept a herd of cattle on the island of Sicily. Odysseus, on his eventful return trip from the Trojan War, earned the wrath of Helios when his starving men killed one of the cattle for food. Archimedes framed his problem around these cattle.

The cattle were of four different colors: white, black,

yellow, and dappled. Some of each color were bulls, some cows. Between the numbers of each color and sex Archimedes set rather easy relationships. For example, if a third and a fourth of the black cattle were grouped together, that collection would total just as many as all the white cows in the god's herds on the island. Archimedes set seven relationships of that sort.

To these seven he added two special requirements. First, the yellow and dappled bulls together formed a triangle. If two bulls were placed side by side behind the first bull, then three behind them, and so on, the whole collection of yellow and dappled bulls would make a triangular shape. Finally, the black and white bulls grouped together formed a square.

How many cattle of the various sorts did Helios graze on the island? No answer has come down from ancient times, so we can't know whether Archimedes or Apollonius solved the problem. Most historians doubt that either of them did.

Modern mathematicians have naturally taken a stab at it. And they have come up with an answer—in fact, two answers. The possibility of two answers comes from the last requirement that the black and white bulls form a square. Does that mean that the total number of them is a perfect square? Possibly. But if you grouped a square number of cattle side by side and head to tail, you would not form a square shape, since cattle are longer than they are wide. Who can be sure what was meant?

One mathematician solved the problem by requiring only that the black and white bulls together form a rectangle. And even with that loose requirement, he found it to be quite a problem. The fewest cattle needed of all colors and sexes together was the grand sum of 5,916,837,175,686—roughly six trillion cattle! The answer is of course preposterous. A simple calculation shows that such a multitude would cover the island with a mound of cattle several hundred layers deep.

If you decide that the number of black and white bulls must be a perfect square, the answer is even more preposterous. With that more difficult requirement, the total number of cattle works out to be a number that starts out with 7,766 and is 206,545 figures long! The Cattle Problem is a demonstration of how an innocent little problem can get out of hand. All of the requirements of the problem can be stated in quite small numbers. Yet the answer comes out immense. Archimedes, it appears, did not have the genius to recognize that his problem was creating more cattle than even the potent Helios could ever have assembled on the fair island of Sicily.

Archimedes' visit to Egypt may have taught him more than the ways of the Alexandrian scientists. It may have taught him the ways of Egyptian farmers. To pump water from the Nile to irrigate their fields, they are reported to have used something called a water drum, which was partly submerged in the river. The drum was partitioned so that when rotated it scooped up water and delivered it to the fields.

Archimedes apparently thought of making the partitions screwlike, which made it possible to raise water through greater distances. In his pump, pockets of water were trapped in the bottom part of each screw turn and carried upward as the pump rotated.

According to reports, Archimedes' screw (see illustration on title page), as the device is now often called, was used to pump bilgewater from the *Lady of Syracuse*. Archimedes' version of the pump had eight twisting passages, matching the eight compartments of the water drum, but later versions commonly had two or three passages. Water screws became widely used in the ancient world. They were usually rotated by a person treading on the barrel that encloses the screw, much as one treads on a treadmill.

29

5

Squaring the Circle

Although tales of his scientific and engineering skill are the best known, Archimedes put much of his energy into mathematics. But most problems that attracted his attention as a mathematician were important to the scientist and engineer as well. One of these was finding the area of a circle.

In these days of calculators, finding the area of a circle is hardly a challenge. Anyone with a scientific calculator in hand needs only to punch in the radius of the circle and then punch a quick sequence of buttons. By some electronic magic, there in the window of the calculator appears the area of the circle in eight figures.

For the ancient Greeks, the job wasn't so simple or the result so accurate. But Archimedes at least improved their plight.

By Archimedes' time, Greek mathematicians had become aware of an important relation for the area of a circle. As was common in those days, they described the relation in terms of shapes. The circle, they decided, has the same area as a special triangle. To construct the triangle of the ancients, you simply draw a rectangle with a width equal to the radius of the circle and a length equal to the circumference and then cut it in half along a diagonal (a line from corner to corner). This relation would be described in different terms today. Since the area of the rectangle is the radius times the circumference, the area of the special triangle is half that much. So the area of a circle is simply half its radius times its circumference. You can see the truth of the relation by looking at a regular polygon (one with equal sides and angles—a square, for example). Think of a line running from the center of the polygon to the center of a side as its radius and the outside boundary as its circumference. By slicing up the polygon much as you would slice a pie (but only along radii or diagonals), you can find that its area is equal to half the radius times the circumference. Since a circle is just a regular polygon with an infinity of sides, the same relation must hold for it too.

Although the ancient Greeks probably arrived at their relation by looking at polygons, they were reluctant to talk about infinity. And so the relation had gone unproved. Archimedes' first contribution was to provide a proof. To satisfy the mathematicians of the day, the ingenious Archimedes did so without ever mentioning infinity.

From a practical point of view, this relation isn't of much use in itself. More often than not, you can't measure both the radius and the circumference of a circle. If you have a circle drawn on a piece of paper, you can easily measure its diameter and from that get the radius. But you will find measuring its circumference with any accuracy a challenge. The triangle of the ancients was an important discovery, but it didn't solve the problem.

The solution could be looked for in two different directions, and Archimedes followed them both. The first direction was of interest to the mathematician in him, the second to the scientist and engineer.

Early mathematicians searched for a solution that used

31

some sort of construction. If you can construct a square having the same area as a circle, you can then easily find the circle's area. You just multiply the sides of the square together. A rectangle or triangle of the same area will of course serve as well as a square.

Searching for a construction that did the job became a mathematical game called "squaring the circle." Like any game, it had some rules, though they were really quite practical ones. You could use only a compass and a straightedge in your construction. Many Greeks before and after Archimedes spent many hours searching in vain for an answer. Only centuries later—after game players of many other lands surely had tried their skill—did mathematicians prove that it can't be done.

The ancients discovered, though, that you can square the circle if you move your straightedge or compass in some steady fashion while drawing a line. One Greek mathematician devised such a scheme in the fifth century B.C. Archimedes discovered another two centuries later.

Archimedes' scheme made use of a curve which has become known as an Archimedean spiral. It is the curve you get if you twirl a compass and at the same time pull the legs farther apart, doing both at a steady rate. With each turn the spiral moves outward the same amount. The groove on a record traces an Archimedean spiral.

Like any good mathematician, once Archimedes had invented his spiral, he looked into all manner of its features. He discovered, for example, how much area is added with each revolution. Among his discoveries was a way to use the spiral to get the area of a circle.

What he did was first draw one of his spirals inside a circle, making it spiral just once from the center to the outside. With that spiral in place he could construct the special triangle that has the same area as the circle.

Archimedes' squaring of the circle, if it could be called that, was really not useful. It was a trick of interest to another mathematician, but it was hardly a help to anyone seeking the area of a circle. The construction, which involves drawing a line that just grazes the spiral, cannot be done accurately. So for Archimedes, following the first direction had been interesting but not productive in any practical sense.

When Archimedes followed the second direction, his success was better. The obvious way to find the area of a circle—at least it seems obvious today—is to make use of *pi*, the ratio

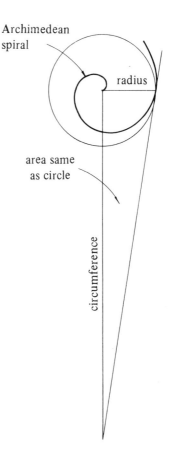

Archimedean spiral

radius

area same as circle

circumference

Archimedes discovered that his spiral could be used to construct a triangle having the same area as a circle.

of circumference to diameter. If you can measure the diameter, you need only multiply by *pi* to get the circumference. You can then easily calculate the area. The only hitch was that the ancients didn't know *pi* accurately. Archimedes decided to do something about that.

The search for *pi* had begun long ago. One of the early estimates of *pi* is found in the Bible. Describing a feature of a temple built by Solomon in the tenth century B.C., one verse says: "He made a molten sea of ten cubits from brim to brim, round in compass . . . and a line of thirty cubits did compass it round about." So the *pi* of the Bible was three.

But many ancient calculators recognized that the circumference of a circle is somewhat more than three times the diameter. As many as a thousand years before the time of Solomon, ancient Babylonians had arrived at a figure of three and an eighth—in decimals, 3.125. The early Egyptians also had a better value. They had decided that the area of a circle was the same as the area of a square that was eight ninths as wide. That gave *pi* a value of three and thirteen eighty-firsts—about 3.16. But all values of *pi,* as far as is known, were just estimates based on measurements. Archimedes was the first to figure out a value mathematically.

Archimedes approached the problem by putting regular polygons inside and outside a circle. He then figured out their perimeters. The perimeter (or circumference) of the circle itself had to lie somewhere in between.

The way his scheme works is easy to see from an example. Put a square inside a circle so that its corners touch the circle. Put another square outside the circle so that its sides touch the circle. If the circle has a diameter of one, it has a circumference of *pi.* The square inside has a perimeter of the square root of eight, or about 2.8. The square outside has a perimeter of 4. So *pi* must lie somewhere between 2.8 and 4.

34

Archimedes, of course, was looking for much better accuracy than squares provide. Instead of a four-sided polygon, he chose one having ninety-six sides. Then he proceeded to find its perimeter both inside and outside a circle. To do that wasn't as easy as it would be today. One thing he had to do was find a value for the square root of three, which was a feat in itself.

In the end Archimedes found he could locate *pi* somewhere between two fairly simple numbers: three and ten seventy-firsts on the low side, and three and a seventh on the high side. In decimals, that's somewhere between about 3.141 and about 3.143.

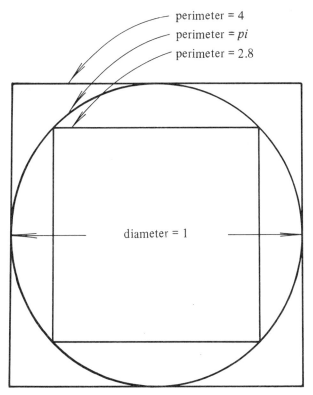

perimeter = 4
perimeter = *pi*
perimeter = 2.8

diameter = 1

Putting limits on *pi*. (Archimedes used ninety-six-sided figures instead of the squares used here.)

Archimedes' answer is good enough for most purposes even today. Many people without *pi* on their calculators are happy to use either 3.14 or else Archimedes' upper limit of three and a seventh (twenty-two sevenths).

Of course, as soon as Archimedes had shown the way, other mathematicians began refining his result. In fact, the first to do so was his rival Apollonius. Over the centuries, other mathematicians put polygons with more and more sides inside and outside a circle. A sixteenth-century Dutch mathematician probably set the record by using polygons with over thirty billion sides. That gave him twenty figures for *pi*— which would seem enough to satisfy anyone.

But it wasn't. In the seventeenth century, mathematicians found quicker ways to calculate *pi*. So the chase went on, adding more and more figures. Eventually, of course, the problem was programmed for a computer. In 1961 one computer spewed out over 100,000 figures for *pi*. In 1967 another yielded 500,000. Naturally, nobody really cared about that many figures. The search Archimedes had started had become a game.

And in mathematics, few games are ever over. In 1986 mathematicians discovered that a superplayer had lived in their midst unnoticed. A young genius from southern India, who died in 1920 at thirty-two, left behind a formula for *pi* that had gone untested for sixty-six years. A computer scientist tried the mysterious formula—its inventor had left no explanation of how he got it—and quickly calculated *pi* to 17 million figures!

6

A Sandy Universe

In the time of Archimedes the naming of numbers hadn't proceeded nearly as far as it has today. When we talk of millions, billions, or trillions, we leave the ancient Greeks far behind. For they named no number larger than our ten thousand, which they called a myriad. Of course, they could talk about larger numbers after a fashion. Our million, for example, was a hundred myriads; our billion was ten myriad myriads. But for very large numbers the language became unwieldly.

Mostly for the sport of it, Archimedes set out to invent a scheme for naming numbers that went beyond the limits of the language then in use. After he devised the scheme, he had to devise a way to use such large numbers, which turned out to be the most interesting part of his work.

Archimedes decided that counting to a myriad myriads—in our numbers, 100 million—was no problem. The ordinary language was good enough for that. A number we would write 12,341,234, for example, the Greeks could easily describe as one thousand, two hundred thirty-four myriad, one thousand, two hundred thirty-four. Numbers in that normal range he called first-order numbers.

To handle numbers larger than a myriad myriads Archimedes defined a new sort of numbers that he called second-order numbers. They were just like first-order numbers except that the step from one number to the next was not one but instead a myriad myriads. A number like 200,003,000 would be expressed as 2 second-order units and 3,000 first-order units. With second-order units, Archimedes could describe numbers as large as ten quadrillion: one followed by sixteen zeros.

Of course, he didn't stop there. The next numbers in the Archimedean scheme were third-order numbers, for which the step between numbers was a myriad myriads of the second-order step. Then followed the fourth order, the fifth, and so on, to the myriad-myriadth order. That gave Archimedes ways to talk about any number up to one followed by eight hundred million zeros—a number big enough for any imaginable use, certainly.

But Archimedes went further. He decided to call all those numbers "period 1" and add to them a "period 2" that started where period 1 left off. Of course, once he started on periods, there was no point in stopping before he had a myriad-myriad periods. The result of all that was a supercollection of numbers that carried Archimedes to a gigantic number equal to one followed by eighty quadrillion zeros. And there he stopped, having gone—it turned out—far beyond any number he would ever have use for.

It is interesting to compare Archimedes' largest number with numbers that have been named since then. In the million-billion-trillion sequence, the biggest number you usually hear about is a centillion, which is one followed by 303 zeros. At least that's what it is to Americans. To the British, who put bigger gaps between named numbers, a centillion is one followed by 600 zeros. Either centillion is far short of Archimedes' number.

But in 1955 Archimedes' number was dethroned. An American mathematician invented a number he called a googol. The googol itself wasn't much: just one followed by one hundred zeros. That's a big number, certainly, but much less even than a centillion. But then for good measure he invented another number: the googolplex. The googolplex was simply one followed by a googol of zeros. And that did it. A googolplex is so large that it's difficult to describe the number of zeros in familiar language. You could say it has ten quindecillion-sexdecillion of them. Or perhaps ten decillion-decillion-decillion would be clearer.

In the long history of mathematics, Archimedes' scheme for describing large numbers never caught on. But it did serve the man himself in one problem that we know about, a problem that he described in a letter to King Hiero's son Gelo.

Some people, suggested Archimedes in his letter, would say that the number of grains of sand is infinite—particularly if you include not only the sands around Syracuse and the rest of Sicily, but also the sands in every region of the world, known or unknown. Others would recognize that the number is not infinite but would be sure that no number is large enough to describe it all. And if we should imagine the earth covered entirely with sand and also fill in the seas and hollows of the earth to the height of the highest mountains, surely no number could be discovered large enough to match such a multitude of sand.

But some of the numbers that he had invented were easily larger than the number of sand grains in such a world, Archimedes wrote to his royal friend Gelo. In fact, he could fill the whole universe entirely with sand and still find a number large enough to match so unbelievable a quantity of sand.

Just to show that he was not trying to make the job easy for himself, Archimedes chose quite a fine sand to use in filling the universe. A space the size of a poppy seed, he decided, would hold a myriad of grains of sand. He put the size of a poppy seed at one fortieth the breadth of a finger. Since a finger's breadth, by Archimedes' units of measure, was about three quarters of an inch (two centimeters), that worked out to be a sand grain of around a thousandth of an inch (about a fiftieth of a millimeter). Just how he decided that was a reasonable size for sand he didn't say. But by today's international soil standards, that's right at the small end of the range of "fine sand."

To most astronomers of Archimedes' day, the sun and the rest of the stars rode on a giant sphere that enclosed the universe. So to attach a size to the universe, Archimedes needed only to know the distance to the sun. And he could figure its distance if he just knew its size.

Several astronomers of the past had reached estimates of the sun's size as compared to the moon's. Eudoxus, who lived a century and more earlier, had decided the sun was nine times as large as the moon. His own father Phidias, Archimedes noted, had arrived at a figure of twelve times as large. But the Alexandrian scientist Aristarchus had shown that the sun was eighteen to twenty times as large. To be on the safe side—he thought—Archimedes supposed the sun to be thirty times as large as the moon. Then, since the earth is surely at least as large as the moon, he decided it was safe to say that the sun is no more than thirty times as large as the earth.

He next needed the size of the earth. Some have shown, Archimedes suggested (rounding off Eratosthenes' figure), that the earth is about 300,000 stades in circumference. Again trying to make his universe big, Archimedes took ten times that size. That gave him an earth with a diameter of about 1,000,000 stades and a sun with a diameter of about 30,000,000 stades.

To find how far away such a sun must lie to appear as it does in the heavens, Archimedes made some measurements.

Up early enough to view the rising sun, he discovered how far from his eye he must hold a small round object so that it just eclipsed the sun. From that he decided that the sun extended between a 656th and an 800th of the way around the horizon. To be on the safe side, Archimedes used a figure of a 1,000th, putting the sun farther away. That made the distance to the sun five billion stades. If Archimedes was using Eratosthenes' value of the stade (a tenth of a mile or a sixth of a kilometer), that amounts to 500 million miles (about 800 million kilometers).

It is interesting that Archimedes' figures did, in the end, overestimate the distance to the sun by about five times. His figure that the sun is 30 times as large as the earth is quite low (it's about 109 times) and would have put the sun too close. His figure that the sun takes up a 1,000th of the horizon made up some of that error (it actually takes up about a 700th). The rest of the distance came from attaching a figure of 3,000,000 stades to the earth's circumference (it's more like 250,000).

Archimedes' distance to the sun gave him a diameter of ten billion stades for his universe, which he now packed with sand. He found he could fill it quite full with a thousand units of the seventh order of the first period of his numbers. In more familiar terms, the number of grains in that immense sphere was one followed by fifty-one zeros.

But Archimedes didn't stop there. He pointed out that his fellow scientist Aristarchus had a different notion of the universe. And if Aristarchus should happen to be right, the universe would be much bigger. Aristarchus, it seems, had suggested that the sun was not located on the sphere of the stars but instead was fixed at the center of that sphere. The earth then revolved around the stationary sun. For this to be true, the stars had to be a great distance from the earth and sun. Otherwise during the year, as the earth orbited the sun, we would notice that we moved closer each month to different regions of the sky, making the stars in that region appear to spread out.

Archimedes decided that Aristarchus's universe needed to be as much bigger than the ordinary universe as the ordinary universe was bigger than the earth. Since the ordinary universe was ten thousand times as big as the earth, Aristarchus's universe must be ten thousand times as big as that. To fill that bigger universe, he quickly decided, required a trillion times as much sand. In Archimedes' numbers that would mean a thousand myriad units of the eighth order, which in modern numbers is one followed by sixty-three zeros.

Even though Archimedes' counting scheme never caught on, his sand play was useful in showing that tremendous numbers can quickly be formed by multiplying smaller numbers together again and again. Today's much simpler idea of multiplying tens together to get larger numbers undoubtedly had its start here in Archimedes' rather unwieldy scheme. His scheme, in fact, immediately inspired his rival Apollonius to invent a handier scheme more like our modern approach.

In the history of ideas, Archimedes' *Sand-Reckoner,* as his letter to Gelo is called, is remembered as much for its ideas about the universe as for its ideas about numbers. Like Archimedes' numbers, Aristarchus's view of the universe should also have been the start of something new. But his notion of a sun-centered universe never took hold and had to be reinvented centuries later by Copernicus.

Archimedes is today never called an astronomer. But he was probably a larger contributor to astronomy than we know about. Both Archimedes and Aristarchus, we learn from others, made some attempt to arrive at a better figure for the length of the year. And according to one writer, Archimedes in some way investigated the distance to the planets.

7

Time of War

Archimedes lived in a time of war between two great powers in the Mediterranean. Rome had come to control much of Italy. Carthage controlled much of the African coast and the islands in the western Mediterranean—including the western part of Sicily. These powers, both anxious to increase their influence, were bound to come to blows sooner or later.

An excuse for combat came in 264 B.C. on the island of Sicily some half a dozen years after King Hiero had come to power. And Hiero himself was much involved. In that year a band of Italian mercenaries who called themselves the Men of Mars seized Messana (now called Messina), a Greek city lying on the narrow strait that separates Sicily from Italy's "toe." They killed or expelled all the male citizens and took over their wives and children for themselves. Once established, they made a living by raiding the nearby Greek cities.

Hiero, whose Syracuse was only 80 miles (130 kilometers) away, tried to put an end to the raids by attacking the ill-gotten city. But the Men of Mars appealed to both Carthage and Rome for help. The Carthaginians arrived first and took over the town, only to be ousted by the later-arriving Romans.

Hiero, no match for either of the powers, yielded first to the Carthaginians, then to the Romans. In the end he made a pact with the victorious Romans. The agreement proved beneficial for both parties. It gave Rome an important source of food, and it gave Syracuse peace and prosperity under the protection of Rome.

But there was no peace between Carthage and Rome. The First Punic War, as their conflict is now called, continued for another two dozen years. In the end Carthage lost most of its fleet and the war. Rome won a sizable payment from defeated Carthage, plus control of Sicily.

The war was to influence the fate of Syracuse for bad as well as good. The Romans had found it necessary to build a fleet, a weapon of war they would eventually use against Syracuse. The fleet was made up mainly of quinqueremes, vessels propelled by five banks of oars. These warships, which would one day test the defenses of Syracuse, were manned by 300 oarsmen. Each could carry 120 fighting men.

The peace between Rome and Carthage was a restless one, and war between the two powers broke out again in 218 B.C. This Second Punic War is remembered for Hannibal's march over the Alps into northern Italy, an invasion that was so successful in its early stages that the future of Rome looked hopeless.

Had Hiero lived, Syracuse might never have been involved in the new conflict. But he died two years after the start of the war, leaving Syracuse in the hands of his grandson. The Carthaginians soon convinced the inexperienced young heir to break with Rome. Although the grandson was assassinated, the leaders who took over were even more anti-Rome.

The change in alliance from Rome to Carthage prepared Syracuse for a sad fate. And sharing in that fate would be

44

Archimedes, who lived on after his longtime friend and king was gone. His king's death, as it happened, would hasten his own.

The Romans began a siege of Syracuse in 215 B.C., three years after the start of the war. It was a unique battle, for it starred two men with quite different talents: a skillful Roman warrior and a skillful Syracusan engineer. The Roman was Marcellus, who had already gained fame for military successes on land and sea. The Syracusan, of course, was Archimedes. It was a contest that would set the ancient world talking for centuries.

Marcellus led the attack from the sea, commanding a fleet of sixty quinqueremes. The vessels were full of men armed either with bows and arrows or with slings and javelins.

Eight of the quinqueremes were specially equipped. Marcellus had created four larger vessels by tying pairs of quinqueremes together side by side with the inside oars removed. On these broader vessels, he installed four-foot-wide shielded ladders that could be raised to carry men to the top of the wall that protected Syracuse. From their appearance, the specially rigged ships were called harps.

As his formidable fleet bore down on Syracuse, Marcellus soon became aware that a genius at warfare had engineered the defense of the city. During the years of peace, King Hiero had asked Archimedes to devise ways to defend Syracuse should attack ever come. Hiero was now dead, but Archimedes was present to direct the use of his machines of war.

When still at a considerable distance, the invading ships were showered with stones and spears flung by catapults behind the walls. The range of the catapults could be shortened as the ships drew nearer, which was unusual in those days. Marcellus soon retreated from the steady barrage and decided to wait for nighttime, when the attackers could reach the wall before being seen. When they were close to the wall, Marcellus reasoned, the missiles from the catapults would fly over their heads.

Marcellus's scheme was successful as far as it went. He was able to approach close enough to avoid the catapults. But he had not counted on Archimedes' ingenuity. For Archimedes had designed loopholes up and down the walls—a new idea, apparently—where archers could stand with their crossbows, protected by the wall, and launch arrows at the invaders.

When a harp approached the wall with its scaling ladder, Archimedes called on another of his engines of war. A beam swung out above the wall, carrying a huge rock dangling from a rope and pulley. Dropped on a harp, the rock demolished the scaling ladder and did serious damage to the ship itself. According to reports, the rocks weighed as much as ten talents, or about 580 pounds (260 kilograms).

The most fantastic—some would say unbelievable—apparatus that Archimedes was supposed to have devised was a crane from which a giant claw was suspended. The claw could be lowered to grasp the prow of a ship and raise it until the vessel sat upright on its stern. Released from the grasp of Archimedes' apparatus, the vessel then capsized or at least shipped a great quantity of water. Marcellus is reported to have complained that Archimedes was using his ships to ladle out the sea.

As if his engines of war weren't spectacular enough, a legend has grown up that Archimedes defended Syracuse against the attack of Marcellus by focusing the sun's rays on his ships and setting them on fire. No report of the siege of Syracuse is from an eyewitness, and so it is hard to know the truth. The earliest source, who described the siege about a century after it happened, made no mention of the burning of ships by any means. Nor did the next two sources, who lived about two and three centuries later. But four centuries after the siege the story surfaced that the crafty Archimedes brought destruction to Marcellus's ships by the use of mirrors. And ever since, historians have been arguing about whether the story could be true.

Archimedes' experience with mathematical shapes could have equipped him to design a focusing mirror. To catch the parallel rays of the sun and bring them to a focus calls for a paraboloid, the same shape that Archimedes used in studying floating objects. So it wouldn't be surprising if Archimedes knew of the usefulness of that shape for focusing. But no writing of his on parabolic reflectors has survived.

That question, though, may be unimportant. A parabolic reflector would probably have been quite impractical. By any estimate, its size would have to be considerable—probably not as large as the giant reflector at Mount Palomar, but still a good-sized structure. More important, it would bring the sun's rays to a focus at only one fixed distance away. To arrange for an enemy ship to be at that distance long enough to burst into flames would seem an impossible task.

A more practical scheme would have been to use a large

Ruins of fortifications that protected Syracuse in Archimedes' time.

47

number of small mirrors in place of a single large one. Then each could be aimed separately. A parabolic reflector, after all, is really nothing more than a collection of exceedingly small mirrors all aimed at the same point.

Public argument about whether Archimedes might have used the sun's rays to set fire to Marcellus's ships began in the seventeenth century, when a famous Italian clashed with a famous Frenchman. A remark by the Italian scientist Galileo showing that he believed the story brought ridicule from the French scientist Descartes, who was sure reflection could not have ignited the ships. Apparently neither scientist made any effort to test the idea.

The first to do so was a seventeenth-century man of the church named Athanasius Kircher. Kircher even went to Syracuse to study the coast where Archimedes must have erected his defenses. Before returning home, he decided that the distance between any reflectors set up by Archimedes and his target was at most thirty paces. So at roughly that distance Kircher focused several mirrors to see how well their effects added together.

His approach was to use five mirrors, adding one at a time. As you would expect, the reflection from one mirror felt much like direct sunlight. Two mirrors gave a noticeably warmer feeling. Three shining on the same spot felt like heat from an open fire. Four gave almost too much heat to bear for any length of time. And the total reflection from five, he reported, could hardly be tolerated at all.

Kircher stopped there, but he decided that he had found a way Archimedes might have pulled off his feat. It remained for another experimenter—as it happened, just a century later—to finish the demonstration that Kircher had started.

Georges Buffon is best known as a naturalist who spent most of his life as director of the Royal Botanical Garden in

Paris. But he became intrigued with the story of Archimedes' burning of the Roman ships. One spring, after some preliminary experimenting, Buffon set up 168 six-by-eight-inch (fifteen-by-twenty-centimeter) glass mirrors in the gardens under his care. After waiting days for the sun to appear, he was finally able to focus the sun's rays on a tarred piece of fir about fifty yards (fifty meters) away. When only 128 of the mirrors were focused, the wood burst into flames. That was enough to convince Buffon that Archimedes could have ignited Marcellus's ships.

Recently a Greek investigator repeated Buffon's experiment with possibly more convincing equipment. He armed fifty to sixty men with polished mirrors about the size of an ancient Greek shield and had them direct the sun's reflection toward a rowboat that had one side covered with the profile of an ancient ship. The mock ship, which was made of tarred plywood, flamed up in about two minutes.

So it is conceivable that Archimedes—or perhaps a large group of Syracusan citizens aiming mirrors or polished shields—set fire to Marcellus's ships by focusing the sun's rays on their wooden structures. But most historians feel it is highly unlikely.

Even though some of Archimedes' defensive tricks could have been exaggerated, his measures were enough to baffle the Romans. One writer reported that the invaders became so terrified that if they spied a rope or small beam extending over the wall, they would turn and flee, fearing that some new device of Archimedes' was appearing to plague them.

Rather than attempt to take Syracuse by storm, Marcellus and his fellow commander, who had attacked the walls of Syracuse from the land with no better success, decided to set up a blockade and starve the city into submission. Archimedes had won the day. But his victory, it turned out, would be in vain.

8

Blood and Sand

Archimedes' defenses were of no help in the eight-month blockade that followed. As it happened, the blockade did not run its course. During negotiations about a captured Syracusan, which brought him near the city, Marcellus noticed that a portion of the wall surrounding Syracuse was poorly guarded. From counting the blocks that lay upon one another to form that portion of the wall, he estimated the height and fashioned two scaling ladders that would reach to the top. Clearly he was not content to wait for starvation to win his contest for him. All he now needed was the right moment for a sneak attack.

That moment arrived soon. In the autumn of the year 212 B.C., Marcellus learned that the Syracusans were celebrating the feast of Artemis, goddess of the hunt. Though prizes from the hunt were not available for the feast—in fact, all food was in short supply because of the blockade—the Syracusans were not short of drink. And on empty stomachs, perhaps the drink had a greater effect.

A force of Marcellus's men raised ladders against the wall

without being noticed and scaled the wall to find the guards in no state to defend their city. The Romans quickly killed the drunk or sleeping guards and took over that part of the city, opening the gates to admit Marcellus and the rest of the men.

The fall of Syracuse was not instantaneous, but in time Marcellus gained the total surrender of the Syracusans. And at the moment of his victory, it is reported, he shed tears at the thought of the coming fate of the beautiful city.

A rule of war in those days was that the fighting men were given the right of plunder after a victory—a sort of payment for a job well done. Against his will—he had little choice—Marcellus agreed to such action.

But Marcellus set down strict rules. Movable property or slaves could be taken. But none of the free citizens of Syracuse were to be killed or raped or enslaved.

The ban, unfortunately, was not wholly successful. The details of its most tragic failure are uncertain. But apparently a soldier came upon Archimedes studying a diagram scratched in the sand. By demanding time to complete his proof, Archimedes seems to have infuriated the soldier, who promptly ran him through with his sword.

A favorite version of the story is that Archimedes was tracing his diagram on a bare patch of sandy ground and shouted at the soldier, "Do not step on my circle!" But several people who have described the scene have suggested that the sand may have been confined to a tray rather than strewn on the ground. Greek mathematicians of those days used a tray full of fine sand as a sort of blackboard. Between uses, the sand could be smoothed to erase the previous problem.

One artist created a mosaic showing Archimedes working at such a tray as a soldier threatens him. The mosaic was supposedly found in the ruins of Herculaneum, one of the cities buried in the eruption of Vesuvius in the first century A.D.

But it was immediately clear to anyone familiar with the way of life in early times that it was not an ancient mosaic. The chair on which Archimedes sat and the table at which he worked were of a sort unknown to the ancients. The fake, one art expert decided, was probably fashioned in the time of Napoleon.

Another version of Archimedes' death suggests that he was hurrying to Marcellus with boxes holding various instruments of mathematics or astronomy. Suspecting the boxes held valuables, the soldier killed him simply for the loot. However caused, Archimedes' killing would seem to have been for the smallest reason.

Marcellus was distressed by the killing of his recent foe. According to reports, he sought out Archimedes' relatives to help and protect them—though what family Archimedes may have left behind, we never learn.

This mosaic picturing Archimedes' death, supposedly buried in the eruption of Vesuvius in the first century A.D., turned out to be a fake.

9

Life after Death

After defeat by Marcellus, Syracuse became another outpost of the spreading Roman Empire. Although it would never again be the glorious city that Hiero ruled, it at least survived the pillage of the Romans. By contrast, the city of Carthage, which later also fell to the Romans (in the Third Punic War), was totally destroyed. After its defeat, Syracuse served for centuries as headquarters for the Roman government of Sicily.

It was undoubtedly government business that brought the Roman lawyer and politician Cicero to the city over a century after Archimedes' death. Cicero, who was active in the politics of Rome at the time of Julius Caesar, had the fortunate habit of writing letters about his experiences, including his stay in Syracuse.

While there, Cicero searched for the tomb of Archimedes and found it sadly neglected. The Roman was distressed that the "once most learned city of Greece" could have allowed the tomb of its most ingenious citizen to be overgrown with brambles. Cicero restored the tomb.

As noted by Cicero, the tomb was easily recognized because of its decoration. Archimedes had asked his friends to mark his tomb with an image of a cylinder surrounding a sphere, and the ratio 3/2. Archimedes, it appeared, regarded finding this ratio as his greatest achievement.

The ratio holds for both area and volume of the two shapes. The area and volume of a cylinder are easily found. The area of a cylinder that's as tall as it is wide is just six times the area of the circle that forms its base. The volume is just the area of its base times its height. But it's not easy to find the area and volume of a sphere. Discovering that all you need to do is multiply the cylinder answers by two thirds was a major achievement.

To discover Archimedes' ratio today, a mathematician would use calculus, a technique developed by Isaac Newton and Gottfried Leibniz in the seventeenth century. Archimedes' method so much resembles calculus that he may deserve some credit for the technique that Newton and Leibniz each sought to claim as his own.

Cicero also reported seeing a planetarium Archimedes had constructed to show the apparent motion of the sun and moon and the five known planets. It was so accurate that it could predict eclipses of the sun and moon if not too far in the future. Made of spheres and possibly run by water, it was at the time considered one of Archimedes' most remarkable achievements.

Following the prevailing view of the time, Archimedes probably placed a stationary earth at the center of his model. That, of course, makes the motion of the planets quite complicated. If Archimedes mimicked that motion in his planetarium, his ingenuity must surely have been challenged. Unfortunately no model or full description survives. We do know that Archimedes wrote an article, now lost, on how to make spheres such as were used in the planetarium.

Archimedes' article about spheres is the only one he ever

wrote about his various contrivances. Historians have often decided that he placed small value on his engineering feats and so didn't bother to write about them. But he could have felt that there was no one to write to. A man such as Conon, who welcomed Archimedes' writings on mathematics, might also be interested in making a planetarium. But schemes for plucking ships from the sea might not interest him. Besides, the need for keeping military schemes secret may have silenced Archimedes.

Cicero was the last to report seeing Archimedes' planetarium or his tomb. No trace of either has been discovered since.

The takeover of Greek cities by the Romans did not end Greek science. With Archimedes gone, Syracuse was no longer a source of new ideas. But Alexandria, home of Eratosthenes and Apollonius, continued to be a gathering place for scientists for half a dozen centuries after Archimedes' death. Progress in mathematics continued, as in astronomy.

Archimedes' work in mechanics and engineering was not picked up immediately, though several centuries later—probably in the third century A.D.—an Alexandrian named Hero behaved enough like the genius of Syracuse to be described by one writer as "a minor Archimedes." He wrote about levers and wedges and pulleys, and experimented with air pressure and with reflection. He invented what may have been the first drink dispenser with a device that spouted water when a coin was fed into a slot. One of his best-known inventions is a steam engine made of a globe fitted with nozzles. The globe was mounted so that it rotated as steam squirted through the nozzles. Like many of his inventions, Hero's engine served more for fun than profit.

Greek science faded as the Roman Empire declined, and interest in the works of Archimedes all but died as the Dark Ages set in. From about the fifth century to the fifteenth, little that could be called science captured the attention of European thinkers.

When interest in science did revive, the work of Archimedes quickly became influential once more. The middle of the sixteenth century saw publication of his more important works. Besides Greek, the works appeared in Latin, which was the language of scientists, and even in Italian. The renewal of interest in Archimedes began in Italy and spread through Europe.

The most important scientist to learn of Archimedes' work was Galileo, whose biggest contribution to science came from his study of motion. Falling or rolling objects, projectiles, and pendulums all attracted his attention. His was the next step in the study of mechanics after Archimedes'. In fact, some historians have wondered why Archimedes himself never took that step. With his interest in missiles, it would have been a natural development.

Some historians have felt that another user of Archimedes' work could have been Copernicus, the man who decided—like Aristarchus—that the earth orbits the sun. Copernicus, they suggested, may have arrived at the notion of a sun-centered universe by seeing Archimedes' *Sand-Reckoner,* which discloses Aristarchus's ideas. But it is now established that Copernicus died the year before Archimedes' work became available.

Unfortunately, not all of Archimedes' writing survived. Just as we learn of Aristarchus's ideas about the motion of the earth through Archimedes, we learn of some of Archimedes' ideas through other writers. We know, for example, that the equation that gives the area of a triangle in terms of its sides was Archimedes' because a writer said he took the equation from a work Archimedes wrote on triangles. From another writer we learn of a lost work on optics but unfortunately almost nothing about what was in it.

You would think that any work of Archimedes' that is now lost must be lost forever. But as recently as 1906 an important lost work was found in a library in Istanbul, Turkey. The work had been copied on parchment in the tenth century, but some time later the owner of the copy had decided to reuse the parchment. He washed out the old writing and proceeded to write a collection of prayers and other religious material over Archimedes' work. But he hadn't done a good job of washing out the old writing, and much of it could still be read.

The most important part of the writing was an item called "Method," which Archimedes had written to Eratosthenes in Alexandria. In it he demonstrated how he solved problems, a question that had puzzled historians. From Archimedes' letter to Eratosthenes, we learn that Archimedes often got an answer in quite a different way than he later proved it. Since his proof was all that he wrote about, his method had been a mystery.

The recovered work also settled a question about a puzzle called the Box of Archimedes. The puzzle was much like the Chinese puzzle called the tangram but with twice as many pieces. It consisted of fourteen ivory pieces that fit together to form a rectangle.

The game was also called the stomachion, which means "something that drives you wild." And trying to put the fourteen pieces back together to form the original rectangle is enough to explain the name. With every piece a different shape, it is like working a blank jigsaw puzzle. As with the tangram, one popular activity with the stomachion was to rearrange the pieces to form a recognizable shape: a geometrical figure, perhaps, or something fanciful like a ship or a tree or a dagger.

Historians had thought that Archimedes' name was attached to the puzzle just as Einstein's name might be attached to a

difficult puzzle today. But the Istanbul parchment showed that
the puzzle was really Archimedes', just as the name indicated.

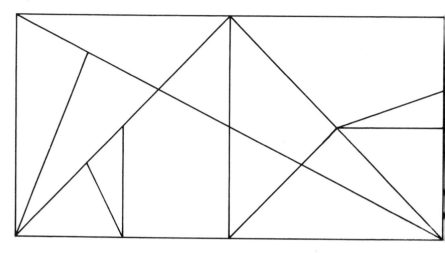

Archimedes' puzzle, when assembled.

If a lost work of Archimedes' can turn up twenty-one centuries after his death, perhaps the story of this greatest scientist of the ancient world will have further chapters. Next year or next century another long-lost work may turn up in another corner of the world. One day some historian browsing in a dusty attic of an ancient library may even come upon a forgotten manuscript labeled "The Autobiography of Archimedes"—in Greek, of course—and we'll learn for the first time something about the private life of this genius among geniuses. And naturally the historian who makes the discovery will dart from the building and run down the street crying, "Eureka!"

Glossary

Archimedes' screw—An inclined screw encased in a tube, designed to raise water when rotated. [also called an Archimedean screw or a water-screw]

block and tackle—An arrangement of rope with blocks containing pulleys, designed to give a mechanical advantage. [also called a tackle]

center of buoyancy—The balance point for the buoyant forces acting on an object.

center of gravity—The balance point for the forces of gravity acting on an object.

circle, ellipse, parabola, hyperbola—These four curves can be formed by cutting a cone. A horizontal cut gives a circle. A cut at an angle less than the cone angle gives an ellipse. A cut at an angle equal to the cone angle gives a parabola. A cut at an angle greater than the cone angle gives a hyperbola.

circumference—The line around a circle, or its length.

cubit—An ancient length based on the distance from the elbow to the fingertips and varying from about 17 to 22 inches (43 to 56 centimeters). Often (as in this book) taken as a foot and a half (or half a meter).

diameter—A straight line running between the edges of a circle through the center, or its length.

ellipse—See circle.

googol—The number 1 followed by a hundred zeroes. [coined by American mathematician Edward Kasner, who died in 1955]

googolplex—The number 1 followed by a googol of zeroes. [also coined by Kasner]

harp—A vessel of ancient warfare formed by joining two quinqueremes side by side and mounting a scaling ladder on their decks.

hyperbola—see circle.

mechanical advantage—An increase in the force coming out of a device (such as a lever or pulley) over the force put in, or the ratio of those forces.

myriad—In ancient times, 10,000 (today, an indefinitely large number).

parabola—See circle.

paraboloid—The surface formed by revolving a parabola on its axis (the line that divides it in half). [more precisely called a paraboloid of revolution]

perimeter—The line around any closed shape, or its length.

pi—The ratio of the circumference to the diameter of a circle. [sixteenth letter of the Greek alphabet]

polygon—A closed shape with straight sides, such as a triangle, square, or pentagon. A "regular" polygon has all sides and angles equal.

quinquereme—An ancient seagoing vessel propelled by five banks of oars.

radius—A straight line from the center to the edge of a circle, or its length.

segment—The shape formed by closing a curve or curved surface (such as a parabola or paraboloid) with a straight line or flat surface. [more precisely called a "right" segment when the closing line or surface is at a right angle to the axis]

specific gravity—The weight of a substance compared to the same volume of water. [more precisely, compared to distilled water at 4 degrees Celsius and normal atmospheric pressure]

spiral—A curve running around a point but getting farther away from the point on each lap. [an Archimedean spiral moves outward the same distance each lap]

stade—An ancient distance based on the length of Greek foot races, often taken as 607 feet (0.115 miles) or 185 meters (0.185 kilometers). Archimedes' contemporary, Eratosthenes, supposedly used a stade of about a tenth of a mile (about a sixth of a kilometer), which is the value used in this book. [also called a stadium or stadion]

stephane—A metal headband that narrows toward the temples, often seen on ancient Greek statues of gods.

stomachion—A puzzle devised by Archimedes made of a rectangle cut into eleven triangles, two quadrilaterals, and a pentagon. [also called the Loculus of Archimedes, the Latin word "loculus" apparently referring to the compartment or box in which the pieces could be put together]

talent—To the ancient Greeks, a unit of weight equal to 6000 drachmas, which amounts to 58 pounds or 26 kilograms. [like the drachma, also used as a unit of money]

tangram—A Chinese puzzle made of a square cut into five triangles, a square, and a parallelogram.

windlass—A lifting or hauling device made of a cylinder wound with a rope or cable and turned by a crank.

worm gear—A screwlike worm meshed with a toothed gear so that turning the worm makes the gear turn, resulting in a large mechanical advantage.

Further Reading

Asimov, Isaac. *Great Ideas of Science*. Boston: Houghton Mifflin, 1969.

Clagett, Marshall. "Archimedes." *Collier's Encyclopedia*, Vol. 2, pp. 479-480. 1988.

Durant, Will. *The Story of Civilization*. Vol. 2, *The Life of Greece*. New York: Simon & Schuster, 1939.

Encyclopedia Americana, Vol. 2, pp. 215-216. 1986.

Gay, Kathlyn. *Science in Ancient Greece*. New York: Franklin Watts, 1988.

Toomer, Gerald J. "Archimedes." *The New Encyclopedia Britannica*, Vol. 13, pp. 930-931. 1988.

Index

A

Alexandria, 9, 24
Apollonius, 27-28, 35, 42
Archimedean spiral, 32, *33*
Archimedes
  birth, 9
  building of ship, 23-24
  death, 9, 51-52, *52*
  defense of Syracuse, 45-49
  father, 9, 40
  moving of ship, 5-8, 24
  test of crown, 12-19
  tomb, 54
  visit to Alexandria, 9, 24, 25-29
  visit to Spain, 9
Archimedes' Principle, 15-16
Archimedes' screw, *1*, 29, 59
Aristarchus, 25-26, 40, 41-42, 56

B

Berenice, 26
block and tackle, 6-8, *7*, 59
Buffon, Georges, 48-49
buoyancy, center of, 21, 59
buoyancy, law of, 15-16
burning
  mirrors, 46-49
  pitch, 9

C

calculus, 54
Cattle Problem, 27-29
centillion, 38
Cicero, 53-55

circle, area of, 30-36
Conon, 26
Copernicus, 56
cubit, 23-24, 59

D

Descartes, 48

E

Eratosthenes, 26-27, 57
Euclid, 25
Eudoxus, 40

G

Galileo, 13-14, 18-19, 48, 56
Gelo, 39
googol, 39, 60
googolplex, 39, 60
gravity, center of, 20-21, 59

H

harp, 45-46
Hero, 55
Hiero II, 5-6, 11-13, 23-24, 43-44, 45

K

Kircher, Athanasius, 48

L

Lady of Alexandria, 24
Lady of Syracuse, 23-24, 29
Leibniz, Gottfried, 54
lever, law of, 19-21

M
Marcellus, 45-52
mechanical advantage, 6, 60
mechanics, 21, 56
Men of Mars, 43
"Method," 57
mosaic, fake, 51-52, *52*
myriad, 37, 60

N
Newton, Issac, 13-14, 54

O
optics, 47, 56
overturning, 21-22, *22*

P
parabola, 20, 27, 60
paraboloid, 20-21, *22*, 47, 60
pi, 33-36, *35*
planetarium, 54
pulley, 6-7
Punic Wars
  First, 43-44
  Second, 44-51
  Third, 53

Q
quinquereme, 44, 45, 60

S
Sand-Reckoner, 42, 56
Sicels, 10
specific gravity, 17, 61
sphere
  area and volume, 54
  construction, 54
stade, 27, 61
stephane, 12, 61
stomachion, 57-58, *58*, 61
Syracuse
  blockade, 50
  fall, 51-52
  location, 9
  modern view, *11*
  origin, 10
  siege, 45-49
  visited by Cicero, 53-55

T
talent, 23, 61
triangle, area of, 56

W
William of Occam, 15
windlass, 8, 24, 61
worm gear, 8, 61